MY ULTIMATE GOAL
PLANNER JOURNAL

THIS JOURNAL BELONGS TO:

_____

BIG GOALS:

GOAL _____

_____

_____

_____

DATE COMPLETED

DATE	STEPS OF ACTIONS	DONE

NOTES

_____

_____

_____

_____

_____

BIG GOALS:

GOAL _____
_____
_____
_____

DATE COMPLETED

DATE	STEPS OF ACTIONS	DONE

NOTES

_____
_____
_____
_____
_____

BIG

GOALS:

GOAL _____
_____
_____
_____

DATE COMPLETED

DATE	STEPS OF ACTIONS	DONE

NOTES

_____
_____
_____
_____
_____

BIG GOALS:

GOAL _____
_____
_____
_____

DATE COMPLETED

DATE	STEPS OF ACTIONS	DONE

NOTES

_____
_____
_____
_____
_____

BIG GOALS:

GOAL _____
_____
_____
_____

DATE COMPLETED

DATE	STEPS OF ACTIONS	DONE

NOTES
_____
_____
_____
_____
_____

BIG GOALS:

GOAL _____
_____
_____

DATE COMPLETED

DATE	STEPS OF ACTIONS	DONE

NOTES

_____
_____
_____
_____
_____

BIG

GOALS:

GOAL _____
_____
_____
_____

DATE COMPLETED

DATE	STEPS OF ACTIONS	DONE

NOTES

_____
_____
_____
_____
_____

BIG GOALS:

GOAL _____
_____
_____
_____

DATE COMPLETED

DATE	STEPS OF ACTIONS	DONE

NOTES

_____
_____
_____
_____
_____

BIG
GOALS:

GOAL _____
_____
_____
_____

DATE COMPLETED

DATE	STEPS OF ACTIONS	DONE

NOTES

_____
_____
_____
_____
_____

BIG GOALS:

GOAL _____
_____
_____
_____

DATE COMPLETED

DATE	STEPS OF ACTIONS	DONE

NOTES

_____
_____
_____
_____
_____

TODAY'S PLAN

DATE: _____

M T W T F S S

HOUR:	PLAN:

TODAY'S GOALS:

1: _____

_____

2: _____

_____

3: _____

_____

TO-DO LIST:

_____ ☐

_____ ☐

_____ ☐

_____ ☐

_____ ☐

_____ ☐

_____ ☐

_____ ☐

TODAY'S PLAN

DATE: _____

M T W T F S S

HOUR:	PLAN:

TODAY'S GOALS:

1: _____

_____

2: _____

_____

3: _____

_____

TO-DO LIST:

_____ ☐

_____ ☐

_____ ☐

_____ ☐

_____ ☐

_____ ☐

_____ ☐

_____ ☐

TODAY'S PLAN

DATE: _____

M T W T F S S

HOUR:	PLAN:

TODAY'S GOALS:

1: _____

_____

2: _____

_____

3: _____

_____

_____

TO-DO LIST:

_____ ☐

_____ ☐

_____ ☐

_____ ☐

_____ ☐

_____ ☐

_____ ☐

_____ ☐

TODAY'S PLAN

DATE: _____

M T W T F S S

HOUR:	PLAN:

TODAY'S GOALS:

1: _____
_____
_____

2: _____
_____

3: _____
_____
_____

TO-DO LIST:

_____ ☐
_____ ☐
_____ ☐
_____ ☐
_____ ☐
_____ ☐
_____ ☐
_____ ☐

TODAY'S PLAN

DATE: _____

M T W T F S S

HOUR:	PLAN:

TODAY'S GOALS:

1: _____

_____

2: _____

_____

3: _____

_____

TO-DO LIST:

_____ ☐

_____ ☐

_____ ☐

_____ ☐

_____ ☐

_____ ☐

_____ ☐

_____ ☐

TODAY'S PLAN

DATE: _____

M T W T F S S

HOUR:	PLAN:

TODAY'S GOALS:

1: _____

_____

2: _____

_____

3: _____

_____

_____

TO-DO LIST:

_____ ☐

_____ ☐

_____ ☐

_____ ☐

_____ ☐

_____ ☐

_____ ☐

_____ ☐

TODAY'S PLAN

DATE: _____

M T W T F S S

HOUR:	PLAN:

TODAY'S GOALS:

1: _____

_____

2: _____

_____

3: _____

_____

_____

TO-DO LIST:

_____ ☐

_____ ☐

_____ ☐

_____ ☐

_____ ☐

_____ ☐

_____ ☐

_____ ☐

TODAY'S PLAN

DATE: _____

M T W T F S S

HOUR:	PLAN:

TODAY'S GOALS:

1: _____

_____

2: _____

_____

3: _____

_____

TO-DO LIST:

_____ ☐

_____ ☐

_____ ☐

_____ ☐

_____ ☐

_____ ☐

_____ ☐

_____ ☐

TODAY'S PLAN

DATE: _____

M T W T F S S

HOUR:	PLAN:

TODAY'S GOALS:

1: _____

_____

2: _____

_____

3: _____

_____

TO-DO LIST:

_____ ☐

_____ ☐

_____ ☐

_____ ☐

_____ ☐

_____ ☐

_____ ☐

_____ ☐

TODAY'S PLAN

DATE: _____

M T W T F S S

HOUR:	PLAN:

TODAY'S GOALS:

1: _____

_____

2: _____

_____

3: _____

_____

TO-DO LIST:

_____ ☐

_____ ☐

_____ ☐

_____ ☐

_____ ☐

_____ ☐

_____ ☐

_____ ☐

TODAY'S PLAN

DATE: _____

M T W T F S S

HOUR:	PLAN:

TODAY'S GOALS:

1: _____

_____

2: _____

_____

3: _____

_____

_____

TO-DO LIST:

_____ ☐

_____ ☐

_____ ☐

_____ ☐

_____ ☐

_____ ☐

_____ ☐

_____ ☐

TODAY'S PLAN

DATE: _____

M T W T F S S

HOUR:	PLAN:

TODAY'S GOALS:

1: _____

_____

2: _____

_____

3: _____

_____

TO-DO LIST:

_____ ☐

_____ ☐

_____ ☐

_____ ☐

_____ ☐

_____ ☐

_____ ☐

_____ ☐

TODAY'S PLAN

DATE: _____

M T W T F S S

HOUR:	PLAN:

TODAY'S GOALS:

1: _____

_____

2: _____

_____

3: _____

_____

TO-DO LIST:

_____ ☐

_____ ☐

_____ ☐

_____ ☐

_____ ☐

_____ ☐

_____ ☐

_____ ☐

TODAY'S PLAN

DATE: _____

M T W T F S S

HOUR:	PLAN:

TODAY'S GOALS:

1: _____
_____

2: _____
_____

3: _____
_____
_____

TO-DO LIST:

_____ ☐
_____ ☐
_____ ☐
_____ ☐
_____ ☐
_____ ☐
_____ ☐
_____ ☐

TODAY'S PLAN

DATE: _____

M T W T F S S

HOUR:	PLAN:

TODAY'S GOALS:

1: _____

_____

2: _____

_____

3: _____

_____

_____

TO-DO LIST:

_____ ☐

_____ ☐

_____ ☐

_____ ☐

_____ ☐

_____ ☐

_____ ☐

_____ ☐

TODAY'S PLAN

DATE: _____

M T W T F S S

HOUR:	PLAN:

TODAY'S GOALS:

1: _____

_____

2: _____

_____

3: _____

_____

_____

TO-DO LIST:

_____ ☐

_____ ☐

_____ ☐

_____ ☐

_____ ☐

_____ ☐

_____ ☐

_____ ☐

TODAY'S PLAN

DATE: _____

M T W T F S S

HOUR:	PLAN:

TODAY'S GOALS:

1: _____

_____

2: _____

_____

3: _____

_____

TO-DO LIST:

_____ ☐

_____ ☐

_____ ☐

_____ ☐

_____ ☐

_____ ☐

_____ ☐

_____ ☐

TODAY'S PLAN

DATE: _____

M T W T F S S

HOUR:	PLAN:

TODAY'S GOALS:

1: _____

_____

2: _____

_____

3: _____

_____

_____

TO-DO LIST:

_____ ☐

_____ ☐

_____ ☐

_____ ☐

_____ ☐

_____ ☐

_____ ☐

_____ ☐

TODAY'S PLAN

DATE: _____

M T W T F S S

HOUR:	PLAN:

TODAY'S GOALS:

1: _____
_____

2: _____
_____

3: _____
_____

TO-DO LIST:

_____ ☐
_____ ☐
_____ ☐
_____ ☐
_____ ☐
_____ ☐
_____ ☐
_____ ☐

TODAY'S PLAN

DATE: _____

M T W T F S S

HOUR:	PLAN:

TODAY'S GOALS:

1: _____
_____
_____

2: _____
_____

3: _____
_____
_____

TO-DO LIST:

_____ ☐
_____ ☐
_____ ☐
_____ ☐
_____ ☐
_____ ☐
_____ ☐
_____ ☐

TODAY'S PLAN

DATE: _____

M T W T F S S

HOUR:	PLAN:

TODAY'S GOALS:

1: _____

_____

2: _____

_____

3: _____

_____

TO-DO LIST:

- _____ ☐
- _____ ☐
- _____ ☐
- _____ ☐
- _____ ☐
- _____ ☐
- _____ ☐
- _____ ☐

TODAY'S PLAN

DATE: _____

M T W T F S S

HOUR:	PLAN:

TODAY'S GOALS:

1: _____

_____

2: _____

_____

3: _____

_____

_____

TO-DO LIST:

_____ ☐

_____ ☐

_____ ☐

_____ ☐

_____ ☐

_____ ☐

_____ ☐

_____ ☐

TODAY'S PLAN

DATE: _____

M T W T F S S

HOUR:	PLAN:

TODAY'S GOALS:

1: _____

_____

2: _____

_____

3: _____

_____

_____

TO-DO LIST:

_____ ☐

_____ ☐

_____ ☐

_____ ☐

_____ ☐

_____ ☐

_____ ☐

_____ ☐

TODAY'S PLAN

DATE: _____

M T W T F S S

HOUR:	PLAN:

TODAY'S GOALS:

1: _____

_____

_____

2: _____

_____

3: _____

_____

_____

TO-DO LIST:

_____ ☐

_____ ☐

_____ ☐

_____ ☐

_____ ☐

_____ ☐

_____ ☐

_____ ☐

TODAY'S PLAN

DATE: _____

M T W T F S S

HOUR:	PLAN:

TODAY'S GOALS:

1: _____

_____

2: _____

_____

3: _____

_____

_____

TO-DO LIST:

_____ ☐

_____ ☐

_____ ☐

_____ ☐

_____ ☐

_____ ☐

_____ ☐

_____ ☐

TODAY'S PLAN

DATE: _____

M T W T F S S

HOUR:	PLAN:

TODAY'S GOALS:

1: _____

_____

2: _____

_____

3: _____

_____

TO-DO LIST:

_____ ☐

_____ ☐

_____ ☐

_____ ☐

_____ ☐

_____ ☐

_____ ☐

_____ ☐

TODAY'S PLAN

DATE: _____

M T W T F S S

HOUR:	PLAN:

TODAY'S GOALS:

1: _____

_____

2: _____

_____

3: _____

_____

TO-DO LIST:

_____ ☐

_____ ☐

_____ ☐

_____ ☐

_____ ☐

_____ ☐

_____ ☐

_____ ☐

TODAY'S PLAN

DATE: _____

M T W T F S S

HOUR:	PLAN:

TODAY'S GOALS:

1: _____
_____
2: _____
_____
3: _____
_____
_____

TO-DO LIST:

_____ ☐
_____ ☐
_____ ☐
_____ ☐
_____ ☐
_____ ☐
_____ ☐
_____ ☐

TODAY'S PLAN

DATE: _____

M T W T F S S

HOUR:	PLAN:

TODAY'S GOALS:

1: _____

_____

2: _____

_____

3: _____

_____

TO-DO LIST:

_____ ☐

_____ ☐

_____ ☐

_____ ☐

_____ ☐

_____ ☐

_____ ☐

_____ ☐

TODAY'S PLAN

DATE: _____

M T W T F S S

HOUR:	PLAN:

TODAY'S GOALS:

1: _____

_____

2: _____

_____

3: _____

_____

TO-DO LIST:

_____ ☐

_____ ☐

_____ ☐

_____ ☐

_____ ☐

_____ ☐

_____ ☐

_____ ☐

TODAY'S PLAN

DATE: _____

M T W T F S S

HOUR:	PLAN:

TODAY'S GOALS:

1: _____
_____

2: _____
_____

3: _____
_____

TO-DO LIST:

_____ ☐
_____ ☐
_____ ☐
_____ ☐
_____ ☐
_____ ☐
_____ ☐
_____ ☐

TODAY'S PLAN

DATE: _____

M T W T F S S

HOUR:	PLAN:

TODAY'S GOALS:

1: _____

_____

2: _____

_____

3: _____

_____

_____

TO-DO LIST:

_____ ☐

_____ ☐

_____ ☐

_____ ☐

_____ ☐

_____ ☐

_____ ☐

_____ ☐

TODAY'S PLAN

DATE: _____

M T W T F S S

HOUR:	PLAN:

TODAY'S GOALS:

1: _____

_____

2: _____

_____

3: _____

_____

_____

TO-DO LIST:

_____ ☐

_____ ☐

_____ ☐

_____ ☐

_____ ☐

_____ ☐

_____ ☐

_____ ☐

TODAY'S PLAN

DATE: _____

M T W T F S S

HOUR:	PLAN:

TODAY'S GOALS:

1: _____

_____

2: _____

_____

3: _____

_____

TO-DO LIST:

_____ ☐

_____ ☐

_____ ☐

_____ ☐

_____ ☐

_____ ☐

_____ ☐

_____ ☐

TODAY'S PLAN

DATE: _____

M T W T F S S

HOUR:	PLAN:

TODAY'S GOALS:

1: _____

_____

2: _____

_____

3: _____

_____

TO-DO LIST:

- _____ ☐
- _____ ☐
- _____ ☐
- _____ ☐
- _____ ☐
- _____ ☐
- _____ ☐
- _____ ☐

TODAY'S PLAN

DATE: _____

M T W T F S S

HOUR:	PLAN:

TODAY'S GOALS:

1: _____

_____

2: _____

_____

3: _____

_____

_____

TO-DO LIST:

_____ ☐

_____ ☐

_____ ☐

_____ ☐

_____ ☐

_____ ☐

_____ ☐

_____ ☐

TODAY'S PLAN

DATE: _____

M T W T F S S

HOUR:	PLAN:

TODAY'S GOALS:

1: _____

_____

2: _____

_____

3: _____

_____

TO-DO LIST:

- _____ ☐
- _____ ☐
- _____ ☐
- _____ ☐
- _____ ☐
- _____ ☐
- _____ ☐
- _____ ☐

TODAY'S PLAN

DATE: _____

M T W T F S S

HOUR:	PLAN:

TODAY'S GOALS:

1: _____

_____

2: _____

_____

3: _____

_____

TO-DO LIST:

_____ ☐

_____ ☐

_____ ☐

_____ ☐

_____ ☐

_____ ☐

_____ ☐

_____ ☐

TODAY'S PLAN

DATE: _____

M T W T F S S

HOUR:	PLAN:

TODAY'S GOALS:

1: _____

_____

2: _____

_____

3: _____

_____

TO-DO LIST:

_____ ☐

_____ ☐

_____ ☐

_____ ☐

_____ ☐

_____ ☐

_____ ☐

_____ ☐

TODAY'S PLAN

DATE: _____

M T W T F S S

HOUR:	PLAN:

TODAY'S GOALS:

1: _____

_____

2: _____

_____

3: _____

_____

TO-DO LIST:

- _____ ☐
- _____ ☐
- _____ ☐
- _____ ☐
- _____ ☐
- _____ ☐
- _____ ☐
- _____ ☐

TODAY'S PLAN

DATE: _____

M T W T F S S

HOUR:	PLAN:

TODAY'S GOALS:

1: _____

_____

2: _____

_____

3: _____

_____

TO-DO LIST:

_____ ☐

_____ ☐

_____ ☐

_____ ☐

_____ ☐

_____ ☐

_____ ☐

_____ ☐

TODAY'S PLAN

DATE: _____

M T W T F S S

HOUR:	PLAN:

TODAY'S GOALS:

1: _____
_____

2: _____
_____

3: _____
_____

TO-DO LIST:

_____ ☐
_____ ☐
_____ ☐
_____ ☐
_____ ☐
_____ ☐
_____ ☐
_____ ☐

TODAY'S PLAN

DATE: _____

M T W T F S S

HOUR:	PLAN:

TODAY'S GOALS:

1: _____

_____

2: _____

_____

3: _____

_____

TO-DO LIST:

_____ ☐

_____ ☐

_____ ☐

_____ ☐

_____ ☐

_____ ☐

_____ ☐

_____ ☐

TODAY'S PLAN

DATE: _____

M T W T F S S

HOUR:	PLAN:

TODAY'S GOALS:

1: _____

_____

2: _____

_____

3: _____

_____

TO-DO LIST:

_____ ☐

_____ ☐

_____ ☐

_____ ☐

_____ ☐

_____ ☐

_____ ☐

_____ ☐

TODAY'S PLAN

DATE: _____

M T W T F S S

HOUR:	PLAN:

TODAY'S GOALS:

1: _____

_____

2: _____

_____

3: _____

_____

TO-DO LIST:

_____ ☐

_____ ☐

_____ ☐

_____ ☐

_____ ☐

_____ ☐

_____ ☐

_____ ☐

TODAY'S PLAN

DATE: _____

M T W T F S S

HOUR:	PLAN:

TODAY'S GOALS:

1: _____

_____

2: _____

_____

3: _____

_____

TO-DO LIST:

_____ ☐

_____ ☐

_____ ☐

_____ ☐

_____ ☐

_____ ☐

_____ ☐

_____ ☐

TODAY'S PLAN

DATE: _____

M T W T F S S

HOUR:	PLAN:

TODAY'S GOALS:

1: _____

_____

2: _____

_____

3: _____

_____

TO-DO LIST:

_____ ☐

_____ ☐

_____ ☐

_____ ☐

_____ ☐

_____ ☐

_____ ☐

_____ ☐

TODAY'S PLAN

DATE: _____

M T W T F S S

HOUR:	PLAN:

TODAY'S GOALS:

1: _____

_____

2: _____

_____

3: _____

_____

_____

TO-DO LIST:

_____ ☐

_____ ☐

_____ ☐

_____ ☐

_____ ☐

_____ ☐

_____ ☐

TODAY'S PLAN

DATE: _____

M T W T F S S

HOUR:	PLAN:

TODAY'S GOALS:

1: _____

_____

2: _____

_____

3: _____

_____

_____

TO-DO LIST:

_____ ☐

_____ ☐

_____ ☐

_____ ☐

_____ ☐

_____ ☐

_____ ☐

_____ ☐

TODAY'S PLAN

DATE: _____

M T W T F S S

HOUR:	PLAN:

TODAY'S GOALS:

1: _____

_____

2: _____

_____

3: _____

_____

TO-DO LIST:

_____ ☐

_____ ☐

_____ ☐

_____ ☐

_____ ☐

_____ ☐

_____ ☐

_____ ☐

TODAY'S PLAN

DATE: _____

M T W T F S S

HOUR:	PLAN:

TODAY'S GOALS:

1: _____

_____

2: _____

_____

3: _____

_____

TO-DO LIST:

_____ ☐

_____ ☐

_____ ☐

_____ ☐

_____ ☐

_____ ☐

_____ ☐

_____ ☐

TODAY'S PLAN

DATE: _____

M T W T F S S

HOUR:	PLAN:

TODAY'S GOALS:

1: _____

_____

2: _____

_____

3: _____

_____

TO-DO LIST:

_____ ☐

_____ ☐

_____ ☐

_____ ☐

_____ ☐

_____ ☐

_____ ☐

_____ ☐

TODAY'S PLAN

DATE: _____

M T W T F S S

HOUR:	PLAN:

TODAY'S GOALS:

1: _____

_____

2: _____

_____

3: _____

_____

TO-DO LIST:

_____ ☐

_____ ☐

_____ ☐

_____ ☐

_____ ☐

_____ ☐

_____ ☐

_____ ☐

TODAY'S PLAN

DATE: _____

M T W T F S S

HOUR:	PLAN:

TODAY'S GOALS:

1: _____
_____

2: _____
_____

3: _____
_____

TO-DO LIST:

_____ ☐
_____ ☐
_____ ☐
_____ ☐
_____ ☐
_____ ☐
_____ ☐
_____ ☐

TODAY'S PLAN

DATE: _____

M T W T F S S

HOUR:	PLAN:

TODAY'S GOALS:

1: _____
_____

2: _____
_____

3: _____
_____

TO-DO LIST:

_____ ☐
_____ ☐
_____ ☐
_____ ☐
_____ ☐
_____ ☐
_____ ☐
_____ ☐

TODAY'S PLAN

DATE: _____

M T W T F S S

HOUR:	PLAN:

TODAY'S GOALS:

1: _____

_____

2: _____

_____

3: _____

_____

TO-DO LIST:

_____ ☐

_____ ☐

_____ ☐

_____ ☐

_____ ☐

_____ ☐

_____ ☐

_____ ☐

TODAY'S PLAN

DATE: _____

M T W T F S S

HOUR:	PLAN:

TODAY'S GOALS:

1: _____

_____

2: _____

_____

3: _____

_____

TO-DO LIST:

_____ ☐
_____ ☐
_____ ☐
_____ ☐
_____ ☐
_____ ☐
_____ ☐
_____ ☐

TODAY'S PLAN

DATE: _____

M T W T F S S

HOUR:	PLAN:

TODAY'S GOALS:

1: _____

_____

2: _____

_____

3: _____

_____

TO-DO LIST:

_____ ☐

_____ ☐

_____ ☐

_____ ☐

_____ ☐

_____ ☐

_____ ☐

_____ ☐

TODAY'S PLAN

DATE: _____

M T W T F S S

HOUR:	PLAN:

TODAY'S GOALS:

1: _____
_____

2: _____
_____

3: _____
_____

TO-DO LIST:

_____ ☐
_____ ☐
_____ ☐
_____ ☐
_____ ☐
_____ ☐
_____ ☐
_____ ☐

TODAY'S PLAN

DATE: _____

M T W T F S S

HOUR:	PLAN:

TODAY'S GOALS:

1: _____

_____

2: _____

_____

3: _____

_____

TO-DO LIST:

_____ ☐

_____ ☐

_____ ☐

_____ ☐

_____ ☐

_____ ☐

_____ ☐

_____ ☐

TODAY'S PLAN

DATE: _____

M T W T F S S

HOUR:	PLAN:

TODAY'S GOALS:

1: _____
_____

2: _____
_____

3: _____
_____

TO-DO LIST:

_____ ☐
_____ ☐
_____ ☐
_____ ☐
_____ ☐
_____ ☐
_____ ☐
_____ ☐

TODAY'S PLAN

DATE: _____

M T W T F S S

HOUR:	PLAN:

TODAY'S GOALS:

1: _____

_____

2: _____

_____

3: _____

_____

_____

TO-DO LIST:

_____ ☐

_____ ☐

_____ ☐

_____ ☐

_____ ☐

_____ ☐

_____ ☐

_____ ☐

TODAY'S PLAN

DATE: _____

M T W T F S S

HOUR:	PLAN:

TODAY'S GOALS:

1: _____

_____

2: _____

_____

3: _____

_____

TO-DO LIST:

_____ ☐

_____ ☐

_____ ☐

_____ ☐

_____ ☐

_____ ☐

_____ ☐

_____ ☐

TODAY'S PLAN

DATE: _____

M T W T F S S

HOUR:	PLAN:

TODAY'S GOALS:

1: _____

_____

2: _____

_____

3: _____

_____

TO-DO LIST:

_____ ☐

_____ ☐

_____ ☐

_____ ☐

_____ ☐

_____ ☐

_____ ☐

_____ ☐

TODAY'S PLAN

DATE: _____

M T W T F S S

HOUR:	PLAN:

TODAY'S GOALS:

1: _____

_____

2: _____

_____

3: _____

_____

TO-DO LIST:

_____ ☐

_____ ☐

_____ ☐

_____ ☐

_____ ☐

_____ ☐

_____ ☐

_____ ☐

TODAY'S PLAN

DATE: _____

M T W T F S S

HOUR:	PLAN:

TODAY'S GOALS:

1: _____

_____

2: _____

_____

3: _____

_____

TO-DO LIST:

_____ ☐

_____ ☐

_____ ☐

_____ ☐

_____ ☐

_____ ☐

_____ ☐

_____ ☐

TODAY'S PLAN

DATE: _____

M T W T F S S

HOUR:	PLAN:

TODAY'S GOALS:

1: _____
_____

2: _____
_____

3: _____
_____

TO-DO LIST:

_____ ☐
_____ ☐
_____ ☐
_____ ☐
_____ ☐
_____ ☐
_____ ☐
_____ ☐

TODAY'S PLAN

DATE: _____

M T W T F S S

HOUR:	PLAN:

TODAY'S GOALS:

1: _____

_____

2: _____

_____

3: _____

_____

_____

TO-DO LIST:

_____ ☐

_____ ☐

_____ ☐

_____ ☐

_____ ☐

_____ ☐

_____ ☐

_____ ☐

TODAY'S PLAN

DATE: _____

M T W T F S S

HOUR:	PLAN:

TODAY'S GOALS:

1: _____

_____

2: _____

_____

3: _____

_____

TO-DO LIST:

_____ ☐

_____ ☐

_____ ☐

_____ ☐

_____ ☐

_____ ☐

_____ ☐

_____ ☐

TODAY'S PLAN

DATE: _____

M T W T F S S

HOUR:	PLAN:

TODAY'S GOALS:

1: _____

_____

2: _____

_____

3: _____

_____

TO-DO LIST:

_____ ☐

_____ ☐

_____ ☐

_____ ☐

_____ ☐

_____ ☐

_____ ☐

_____ ☐

TODAY'S PLAN

DATE: _____

M T W T F S S

HOUR:	PLAN:

TODAY'S GOALS:

1: _____

_____

2: _____

_____

3: _____

_____

TO-DO LIST:

_____ ☐

_____ ☐

_____ ☐

_____ ☐

_____ ☐

_____ ☐

_____ ☐

_____ ☐

TODAY'S PLAN

DATE: _____

M T W T F S S

HOUR:	PLAN:

TODAY'S GOALS:

1: _____

_____

2: _____

_____

3: _____

_____

TO-DO LIST:

_____ ☐

_____ ☐

_____ ☐

_____ ☐

_____ ☐

_____ ☐

_____ ☐

_____ ☐

TODAY'S PLAN

DATE: _____

M T W T F S S

HOUR:	PLAN:

TODAY'S GOALS:

1: _____

_____

2: _____

_____

3: _____

_____

TO-DO LIST:

- ☐
- ☐
- ☐
- ☐
- ☐
- ☐
- ☐
- ☐

TODAY'S PLAN

DATE: _____

M T W T F S S

HOUR:	PLAN:

TODAY'S GOALS:

1: _____
_____

2: _____
_____

3: _____
_____

TO-DO LIST:

_____ ☐
_____ ☐
_____ ☐
_____ ☐
_____ ☐
_____ ☐
_____ ☐

TODAY'S PLAN

DATE: _____

M T W T F S S

HOUR:	PLAN:

TODAY'S GOALS:

1: _____

_____

2: _____

_____

3: _____

_____

TO-DO LIST:

- _____ ☐
- _____ ☐
- _____ ☐
- _____ ☐
- _____ ☐
- _____ ☐
- _____ ☐
- _____ ☐

TODAY'S PLAN

DATE: _____

M T W T F S S

HOUR:	PLAN:

TODAY'S GOALS:

1: _____

_____

2: _____

_____

3: _____

_____

_____

TO-DO LIST:

_____ ☐

_____ ☐

_____ ☐

_____ ☐

_____ ☐

_____ ☐

_____ ☐

_____ ☐

TODAY'S PLAN

DATE: _____

M T W T F S S

HOUR:	PLAN:

TODAY'S GOALS:

1: _____

_____

2: _____

_____

3: _____

_____

TO-DO LIST:

_____ ☐

_____ ☐

_____ ☐

_____ ☐

_____ ☐

_____ ☐

_____ ☐

_____ ☐

TODAY'S PLAN

DATE: _____

M T W T F S S

HOUR:	PLAN:

TODAY'S GOALS:

1: _____
_____
_____

2: _____
_____
_____

3: _____
_____
_____

TO-DO LIST:

_____ ☐

_____ ☐

_____ ☐

_____ ☐

_____ ☐

_____ ☐

_____ ☐

_____ ☐

TODAY'S PLAN

DATE: _____

M T W T F S S

HOUR:	PLAN:

TODAY'S GOALS:

1: _____

_____

2: _____

_____

3: _____

_____

TO-DO LIST:

_____ ☐

_____ ☐

_____ ☐

_____ ☐

_____ ☐

_____ ☐

_____ ☐

_____ ☐

TODAY'S PLAN

DATE: _____

M T W T F S S

HOUR:	PLAN:

TODAY'S GOALS:

1: _____

_____

2: _____

_____

3: _____

_____

_____

TO-DO LIST:

_____ ☐

_____ ☐

_____ ☐

_____ ☐

_____ ☐

_____ ☐

_____ ☐

_____ ☐

TODAY'S PLAN

DATE: _____

M T W T F S S

HOUR:	PLAN:

TODAY'S GOALS:

1: _____

_____

2: _____

_____

3: _____

_____

TO-DO LIST:

_____ ☐

_____ ☐

_____ ☐

_____ ☐

_____ ☐

_____ ☐

_____ ☐

_____ ☐

TODAY'S PLAN

DATE: _____

M T W T F S S

HOUR:	PLAN:

TODAY'S GOALS:

1: _____
_____

2: _____
_____

3: _____
_____

TO-DO LIST:

_____ ☐
_____ ☐
_____ ☐
_____ ☐
_____ ☐
_____ ☐
_____ ☐
_____ ☐

TODAY'S PLAN

DATE: _____

M T W T F S S

HOUR:	PLAN:

TODAY'S GOALS:

1: _____
_____

2: _____
_____

3: _____
_____

TO-DO LIST:

_____ ☐
_____ ☐
_____ ☐
_____ ☐
_____ ☐
_____ ☐
_____ ☐
_____ ☐

TODAY'S PLAN

DATE: _____

M T W T F S S

HOUR:	PLAN:

TODAY'S GOALS:

1: _____

_____

2: _____

_____

3: _____

_____

_____

TO-DO LIST:

_____ ☐

_____ ☐

_____ ☐

_____ ☐

_____ ☐

_____ ☐

_____ ☐

_____ ☐

TODAY'S PLAN

DATE: _____

M T W T F S S

HOUR:	PLAN:

TODAY'S GOALS:

1: _____

_____

2: _____

_____

3: _____

_____

TO-DO LIST:

_____ ☐

_____ ☐

_____ ☐

_____ ☐

_____ ☐

_____ ☐

_____ ☐

_____ ☐

TODAY'S PLAN

DATE: _____

M T W T F S S

HOUR:	PLAN:

TODAY'S GOALS:

1: _____

_____

2: _____

_____

3: _____

_____

_____

TO-DO LIST:

_____ ☐

_____ ☐

_____ ☐

_____ ☐

_____ ☐

_____ ☐

_____ ☐

_____ ☐

TODAY'S PLAN

DATE: _____

M T W T F S S

HOUR:	PLAN:

TODAY'S GOALS:

1: _____

_____

2: _____

_____

3: _____

_____

TO-DO LIST:

_____ ☐

_____ ☐

_____ ☐

_____ ☐

_____ ☐

_____ ☐

_____ ☐

_____ ☐

TODAY'S PLAN

DATE: _____

M T W T F S S

HOUR:	PLAN:

TODAY'S GOALS:

1: _____

_____

2: _____

_____

2: _____

_____

TO-DO LIST:

_____ ☐

_____ ☐

_____ ☐

_____ ☐

_____ ☐

_____ ☐

_____ ☐

_____ ☐

TODAY'S PLAN

DATE: _____

M T W T F S S

HOUR:	PLAN:

TODAY'S GOALS:

1: _____

_____

2: _____

_____

3: _____

_____

TO-DO LIST:

_____ ☐

_____ ☐

_____ ☐

_____ ☐

_____ ☐

_____ ☐

_____ ☐

_____ ☐

TODAY'S PLAN

DATE: _____

M T W T F S S

HOUR:	PLAN:

TODAY'S GOALS:

1: _____
_____

2: _____
_____

3: _____
_____

TO-DO LIST:

_____ ☐
_____ ☐
_____ ☐
_____ ☐
_____ ☐
_____ ☐
_____ ☐
_____ ☐

TODAY'S PLAN

DATE: _____

M T W T F S S

HOUR:	PLAN:

TODAY'S GOALS:

1: _____

_____

2: _____

_____

3: _____

_____

TO-DO LIST:

_____ ☐

_____ ☐

_____ ☐

_____ ☐

_____ ☐

_____ ☐

_____ ☐

_____ ☐

TODAY'S PLAN

DATE: _____

M T W T F S S

HOUR:	PLAN:

TODAY'S GOALS:

1: _____

_____

2: _____

_____

3: _____

_____

TO-DO LIST:

_____ ☐

_____ ☐

_____ ☐

_____ ☐

_____ ☐

_____ ☐

_____ ☐

_____ ☐

TODAY'S PLAN

DATE: _____

M T W T F S S

HOUR:	PLAN:

TODAY'S GOALS:

1: _____

_____

2: _____

_____

3: _____

_____

TO-DO LIST:

_____ ☐

_____ ☐

_____ ☐

_____ ☐

_____ ☐

_____ ☐

_____ ☐

_____ ☐

TODAY'S PLAN

DATE: _____

M T W T F S S

HOUR:	PLAN:

TODAY'S GOALS:

1: _____

_____

2: _____

_____

3: _____

_____

TO-DO LIST:

_____ ☐

_____ ☐

_____ ☐

_____ ☐

_____ ☐

_____ ☐

_____ ☐

_____ ☐

TODAY'S PLAN

DATE: _____

M T W T F S S

HOUR:	PLAN:

TODAY'S GOALS:

1: _____

_____

2: _____

_____

3: _____

_____

TO-DO LIST:

_____ ☐

_____ ☐

_____ ☐

_____ ☐

_____ ☐

_____ ☐

_____ ☐

_____ ☐

TODAY'S PLAN

DATE: _____

M T W T F S S

HOUR:	PLAN:

TODAY'S GOALS:

1: _____

_____

2: _____

_____

3: _____

_____

TO-DO LIST:

_____ ☐

_____ ☐

_____ ☐

_____ ☐

_____ ☐

_____ ☐

_____ ☐

_____ ☐

TODAY'S PLAN

DATE: _____

M T W T F S S

HOUR:	PLAN:

TODAY'S GOALS:

1: _____

_____

2: _____

_____

3: _____

_____

TO-DO LIST:

_____ ☐

_____ ☐

_____ ☐

_____ ☐

_____ ☐

_____ ☐

_____ ☐

_____ ☐

TODAY'S PLAN

DATE: _____

M T W T F S S

HOUR:	PLAN:

TODAY'S GOALS:

1: _____

_____

2: _____

_____

3: _____

_____

_____

TO-DO LIST:

_____ ☐

_____ ☐

_____ ☐

_____ ☐

_____ ☐

_____ ☐

_____ ☐

_____ ☐

TODAY'S PLAN

DATE: _____

M T W T F S S

HOUR:	PLAN:

TODAY'S GOALS:

1: _____

_____

2: _____

_____

3: _____

_____

TO-DO LIST:

- [ ] _____
- [ ] _____
- [ ] _____
- [ ] _____
- [ ] _____
- [ ] _____
- [ ] _____
- [ ] _____

TODAY'S PLAN

DATE: _____

M T W T F S S

HOUR:	PLAN:

TODAY'S GOALS:

1: _____

_____

2: _____

_____

3: _____

_____

TO-DO LIST:

_____ ☐

_____ ☐

_____ ☐

_____ ☐

_____ ☐

_____ ☐

_____ ☐

_____ ☐

TODAY'S PLAN

DATE: _____

M T W T F S S

HOUR:	PLAN:

TODAY'S GOALS:

1: _____

_____

2: _____

_____

3: _____

_____

_____

TO-DO LIST:

_____ ☐

_____ ☐

_____ ☐

_____ ☐

_____ ☐

_____ ☐

_____ ☐

_____ ☐

TODAY'S PLAN

DATE: _____

M T W T F S S

HOUR:	PLAN:

TODAY'S GOALS:

1: _____

_____

2: _____

_____

3: _____

_____

TO-DO LIST:

_____ ☐

_____ ☐

_____ ☐

_____ ☐

_____ ☐

_____ ☐

_____ ☐

_____ ☐

TODAY'S PLAN

DATE: _____

M T W T F S S

HOUR:	PLAN:

TODAY'S GOALS:

1: _____
_____

2: _____
_____

3: _____
_____

TO-DO LIST:

_____ ☐
_____ ☐
_____ ☐
_____ ☐
_____ ☐
_____ ☐
_____ ☐
_____ ☐

TODAY'S PLAN

DATE: _____

M T W T F S S

HOUR:	PLAN:

TODAY'S GOALS:

1: _____
_____

2: _____
_____

3: _____
_____

TO-DO LIST:

_____ ☐
_____ ☐
_____ ☐
_____ ☐
_____ ☐
_____ ☐
_____ ☐
_____ ☐

Made in the USA
Columbia, SC
15 October 2023

24494732R00065